EXISTENTIALISM
NOW

EXISTENTIALISM
NOW

Realizing the Dream of
a Whole Self

CHRISTOPHER BEK

ARPress
45 Dan Road Suite 5
Canton MA 02021

Hotline: 1(888) 821-0229
Fax: 1(508) 545-7580

Ordering Information:
Quantity sales. Special discounts are available on quantity purchases by corporations, associations, and others. For details, contact the publisher at the address above.

Printed in the United States of America.

ISBN-13:	Paperback	979-8-89389-951-1
	eBook	979-8-89389-950-4

Library of Congress Control Number: 2024920133

TABLE OF CONTENTS

TESTIMONIALS

There can be no other truth to take off from than this: I think, therefore I exist [i.e., the Cartesian cogito]. There we have the absolute truth of consciousness becoming aware of itself. Every theory which takes man out of the moment in which he becomes aware of himself is, at its very beginning, a theory which confounds the truth, for outside the Cartesian cogito, all views are only probable, and a doctrine of probability which is not bound to a truth dissolves into thin air. In order to describe the probable, you must have a firm hold on the true. Therefore, before there can be any truth whatsoever, there must be an absolute truth; and this one is easily arrived at; it is on every-one's doorstep; it is a matter of grasping it directly.

—Jean-Paul Sartre

Let our students of philosophy enter the world with no favor shown them; they shall compete with men of brawn and men of cunning; in the mart of strife they shall learn from the book of life itself; they shall hurt their fingers and scratch their philosophic shins on the crude realities of the world; they shall earn their bread and butter by the sweat of their brows. This last and sharpest test shall go on ruthlessly for fifteen long years. Those that survive, scarred and fifty, sobered and self-reliant, shorn of scholastic vanity by the merciless friction of life, and armed now with all the wisdom that tradition and experience, culture and conflict, can cooperate to give. These men at last shall become our leaders.

　—*Will Durant*

The existentialist is first and foremost an individual who is in an infinite relationship with himself and his destiny.

　—*Jean Wahl*

INTRODUCTION

In 1995, I got three pups and named them Camus, Copper, and Kafka. I soon realized that three was too many, and I gave Kafka away to a retirement home. I called them by their names often and treated them as individuals. Camus and Copper were happy dogs with unique personalities. I believe they were self-aware. Camus was an existentialist, and Copper was more elemental than existential. I taught them to cross the street on command, which made our long walks to the coffee shops great fun. My dogs inspired me philosophically and scientifically with the uncomplicated way in which they saw reality. I posted their pictures on my Philosophy Magazine website so they can find their way back to me when they reincarnate.

Plato founded philosophy by daring to ask what existence would be like outside the cave. Philosophy Magazine endeavours to support those who have taken the road less travelled in the struggle towards daylight. Philosophy Magazine is philosophy and science for the third millennium. It represents a whole new way of looking at the universe and our place in it. The theory of one puts a frame of reference around the universe, and this book localizes our existence within the universe.

I am a mathematician, actuary, philosopher, scientist, and published writer; I am also a superior spreadsheet, database, and risk-modeling craftsman. I have consulted to the top executives of one of the largest companies in Canada (Canadian Pacific Limited), and I have made presentations relating to the philosophy and science of risk management in Houston and New York. I founded Philosophy Magazine.com on January 1, 2001. I have lived and worked in Toronto, San Francisco, and my hometown of Calgary.

Starting with my "The Theory of One" essay in 2001, I have written essays on a wide range of subjects, including relativity theory, quantum theory, portfolio theory, existentialism, ontology, paradigm shifts, art and moral choice, the illusion of reality, schizophrenia, and determinism and free will. In 2015, I published an amazing little book entitled *The Theory of One: Realizing the Dream of a Final Theory*. The *Theory of One* proves that physicists cannot be trusted to tell the truth, while *Existentialism Now* proves that doctors cannot be trusted to tell the truth.

A friend recommended that this be thought of as a book of seven essays. Each of the seven essays could be considered and understood in isolation. While it is certainly desirable for the reader to reach critical mass and comprehend the whole book from thirty thousand feet, I believe that comprehension starts with the individual essay. Seven letters become a word. Seven words become a sentence. Seven sentences become a paragraph. Seven paragraphs become an essay. Seven essays become a book. Two books become a paradigm shift.

I believe the problem with the system is behaviourism and the solution is existentialism. Behaviourism only asks that we behave ourselves. It denies any human reality beyond material appearances. Alternatively, existentialism is focused on the workings of consciousness and becoming self-aware. It concerns itself with freedom, responsibility, subjective choice, and human emotions. I would like to see existentialism taught in high schools. I contend that if we were to embrace existentialism holistically as a society, we could sit back and watch the world change overnight.

CARTESIAN METHOD OF READING

René Descartes (1596–1650) was a French scientist, mathematician, and father of modern philosophy. He began his philosophic quest for certainty by tearing down the medieval house of knowledge and then building again from the ground up. Descartes employed the method of radical doubt when he asked the simple question: "What do I know for certain?" He concluded that he certainly knew of his own existence, which he then immortalized with his celebrated *cogito*—i.e., *cogito, ergo sum* (I think, therefore I exist). And following Descartes' lead, *Existentialism Now* takes the reader on a fantastic quest for self-certainty. Here the responsibility of the reader lies simply in embracing the ideas as the null hypothesis for the brief time it takes to read this book. After having accepted the ideas for a time, the prudent reader will then be properly positioned to accept or reject existentialism with certainty once and for all.

Descartes expressly advocates the option-based approach to reading. Accordingly, the first pass is strictly experiential, like driving a convertible sports car along a mountain road on one of the last days of summer. The goal here is simply to keep the car on the road. The second pass requires a more careful reading and asks that the reader mark pertinent passages and make plenty of notes in the margins. The third and final pass calls for the rereading of notes and marked passages. The Cartesian method provides the option of forgoing the second and third readings while, at the same time, still affording the reader a good basic sense of the book.

I encourage my readers to follow Descartes' approach for reading this book, which has been carefully written for the cultured public. It is intended as a two-hour luxury vacation through the brave new world of onespace for both students and anyone interested in philosophy and science. "Onespace" is a metaphysical place where everything is simple, beautiful, and reasonable. For convenience, the book has been specifically designed to comfortably fit inside a coat pocket so that it travels well.

Essay One:
An Existential Life

This *essay tells the story of my existential life and what I have learned from it, as discussed in the three appendices.*

Just listened to Chris's story . . . wonderful, inspiring! So much to be proud of here.

—Sandra Jansen, MLA

T HE 1999 MOVIE *Three Kings* tells a story that took place in the aftermath of the Persian Gulf War. Four American soldiers set out to steal gold that had been stolen from Kuwait, but they also found people who desperately needed their help. Upon preparing to rescue a fallen comrade from an Iraqi bunker, the commander advised one of his soldiers, "You do the thing you are most afraid of—and then you get the courage afterwards." Existentialism means having the courage to take responsibility and to live life on one's own terms.

I was born in Edmonton to a family of six. I had a positive childhood where we lived in nice houses and always had good food on the table. In the summers, we would go to our cabin at Pigeon Lake where we would waterski and spend time with our extended family. It was the highlight of my youth. When I was eleven, my family moved to Calgary when my father was transferred there with Esso, where he worked for thirty-seven years. I always did all right in school and still enjoy the idea of taking complicated ideas and making them simple. After graduating from high school, I went on to the University of Calgary and graduated with a bachelor of science degree in applied mathematics.

I then moved to Toronto and started working for an actuarial consulting firm called The Wyatt Company, where I conducted actuarial science work in valuing pension plans. I very much enjoyed working at Wyatt, but I became homesick and moved back to Calgary. I continued working with Wyatt, but I changed over from pensions to risk management. I mathematically valued losses for risk factors like property, liability, and business interruption. Everything was going well, and I was even able to buy my dream house in Crescent Heights in Calgary. After a few years at Wyatt, I started my own consulting firm, Risk Management Services, which became quite successful. I was offering a whole new perspective on holistic risk management, which involved taking a view from the top. I developed leading-edge mathematical and qualitative models involving risk management and portfolio theory. I consulted to many large organizations, including TransCanada PipeLines, NOVA Corporation, and Petro-Canada. My biggest client was the CFO and treasurer of Canadian Pacific Limited (CPL).

I produced twenty essays of my newly minted publication, the *Risk Management Review*, largely based on the connection between physics and finance. For a few years, I sent out my publications to thirty-six oil and gas executives. As I went forward, my writing started to drift towards philosophy and science, so I decommissioned the *Risk Management Review* and created *Philosophy Magazine*, which is about philosophy and science for the third millennium. The philosophy is primarily existentialism (see Appendix 2) and the science is primarily the theory of one (see Appendix 1) and the Bernoulli Model, which is an advanced application of portfolio theory that takes a top-down view of corporate finance (see Appendix 3). I formulated the basis of my theory of one in 2000 and launched PhilosophyMagazine.com on January 1, 2001, which included the first draft of my theory based on one argument. The 2015 published version of my book is based on seven arguments. I have since written eighty-eight essays for *Philosophy Magazine* that I post to my website and mail out to seventy people around the world every month.

After spending three years at CPL, the company broke up into its five subsidiaries. At the same time, I posted my theory of one essays to PhilosophyMagazine.com. I presented my theory of one to the CFO and treasurer, but they were far too busy with the breakup of the company. And as a result of the breakup, I was out of work. I have come to realize that because of the incredible magnitude of my theory, change occurs at a glacially slow rate, and it was unfair to ask them to care. Even now, eighteen years later, I am still swimming upstream. Losing my biggest client and not having anyone to care about my astonishing theory was extremely hard to take. I met with my doctor and told him I was having suicidal thoughts. My argument was that if nobody cares about the truth, then what is the point of living? But that was a long time ago, and I have evolved greatly since then so that I dauntlessly search for truth and refuse to let things get complicated.

Carrying on from CPL, I developed the aforementioned Bernoulli Model. Unfortunately, I was unable to find any interested companies. I then decided to stop trying to consult and focused all my attention on my theory and writing essays and letters to the government. I was beginning to have some mental health challenges and ended up in the hospital on four occasions. During this time, I came up with the following argument: Consider how the Canadian Constitution "recognizes the supremacy of God," and how Einstein once claimed, "God is the sum total of the laws of nature." This implies that the laws of nature are supreme to everything, including the laws of the government. In other words, the laws of nature trump the laws of the government. Relativity theory, quantum theory, and my own theory of one are all laws of nature. I would thus argue that the government has no legal right to take action against me while I have an outstanding claim for a law of nature. I sacrificed my house to make this point.

Over the years, I have served up one eternal truth after another—but no one cares. With no income, I was unable to pay my mortgage, and my dream home was taken away from me. With nowhere to go, my mother brought me to the hospital where I stayed for a year. While in the hospital I was diagnosed with schizophrenia. It was a difficult illness to understand, until I discovered the origin of the word comes from ancient Greece and simply means "divided mind."

After my stay in the hospital I moved to a group home for another year and was connected to the Canadian Mental Health Association (CMHA). Working with CMHA, they determined I was stable enough to live independently and referred me to Horizon Housing, which provides affordable housing to people in need. As soon as I walked into my new Horizon apartment, I said, "I will take it!" I did not even have to look around; it just felt like home.

It is easy to take things for granted in our lives, but I'm proof that life's circumstances can change. And yes, although I miss my old house and my dogs, I love my apartment. As far as I am concerned, I am living like a king. I have everything I need—a stereo, television, computer, and five hundred books on philosophy and science. I honestly do not know where I would be today without my apartment. I live in a stress-free environment where I can deal with my mental health issues and focus on my passions of reading books, writing essays and books, and communicating with others about my work.

Conclusion

I would like to thank the government for supporting me all these years. I would, however, point out that had they answered my theory of one and existentialism points in the first place, I would never have become sick. But we know from Nietzsche that sickness is a gift for us to overcome. I have overcome schizophrenia, and I have produced gifts, such as my two books and eighty-eight essays—one of which is called *Curing Schizophrenia*.

Appendix 1: The Theory of One

I originally posted my theory of one to PhilosophyMagazine.com in 2001. I published *The Theory of One* book in 2015. My theory solves the greatest scientific problem of all time by uniting relativity theory (1905) with quantum theory (1925). Light speed (the speed limit inside the universe) and Planck's constant (a very small indivisible unit of energy) are the two major universal constants. Relativity theory is based on light speed, and quantum theory is based on Planck's constant. My theory unites these two theories by recognizing that light speed and Planck's constant are the same boundary of the spacetime continuum. In addition to proving that the universe is bounded, it also proves there is only one photon (a being of light); that one photon is God (the Bible also says that God is light), and that reality is an illusion—meaning, the moon does not exist. The theory of one also tracks all the way back to the Big Bang, where the God-photon produced a primordial particle in God's womb that split into an electron (matter) and a positron (antimatter); this was the moment of the Big Bang, and the resulting universe still exists inside the Godphoton today.

APPENDIX 2: EXISTENTIALISM

The behavioural psychological model is used exclusively in Canada, and it only asks that we behave normally. Behaviourism is the theory that observable, objective activities can provide a proper representation of human behaviour. It is the sickness that pervades our society. Existentialism cures behaviourism by asking each of us to take responsibility for the world. It gives us meaning to our lives. Existentialism is primarily the work of some of the great nineteenth-and twentieth-century European philosophers, including Kierkegaard, Nietzsche, Dostoyevsky, Kafka, Camus, and Sartre. They all shared the belief that philosophy begins with the concrete human experience—that is, with the acting, feeling, and living human being. Existentialism also concerns itself with bad faith (i.e., failing to take responsibility) and its opposite, authenticity; authenticity is the degree to which one's true nature, spirit, and character exist in reality despite the overwhelming social pressure to conform.

Appendix 3: The Bernoulli Model

The Bernoulli Model takes portfolio theory to the next level, bringing all moving parts into a single portfolio distribution, like the normal distribution. I spent a year developing the Bernoulli Model. It uses a top-down, strategic management approach to scientific management and combines the processes of forecasting, integrating, and optimizing. The Bernoulli Model employs the forecasting method of Monte Carlo simulation along with the four-moment Camus distribution, which I developed in order to model the full spectrum of risk factors like property, liability, and pension funding. The factors are then integrated by calculating the four moments of the simulated outcome. Optimization algorithms then search risk-reward space in order to determine optimal decisions subject to Delphi constraints. The Delphi is an iterative questionnaire used to identify fundamental organizational values.

ESSAY TWO:
EXISTENTIALISM IN TEN MINUTES

This essay defines existentialism and then describes the ideas of six major existentialists and their major written works.

The essential consequence of existentialism is that man, being condemned to be free, carries the weight of the whole world on his shoulders. He is responsible for the world and for himself as a way of being.

—Jean-Paul Sartre

AS MENTIONED IN the previous essay, the Canadian Constitution recognizes the supremacy of God. The Canadian Charter of Rights and Freedoms became constitutionally entrenched in 1982; it is prefaced as follows: "Canada is founded upon principles that recognize the supremacy of God and the rule of law." Albert Einstein said that God is the sum total of the laws of nature. I have sent letters to the Canadian government claiming they had no legal right to let the bank take my house in that it violates the Constitution. One chooses to become an existentialist by taking responsibility. By holding true to my arguments, I am an existentialist proving that the government has not taken responsibility and is acting in bad faith (which I explain more in "Essay Four: Applied Existentialism").

DEFINING EXISTENTIALISM

Kierkegaard initiated existentialism in the early nineteenth century, and it effectively died with Sartre in 1980—although it has had a resurgence over the past few years. It is the philosophy emphasizing individual existence, freedom and choice. Existentialism stresses that each individual has total freedom and total responsibility for the entire world. For man, existentialism tells us that existence precedes essence. Consider a pen for example. Its essence (i.e., its design) comes before its existence. Alternatively, man arrives on the scene (i.e., his existence) then creates his essence. Consider that the Freudian cognitive model has the ego choosing between the id (or self or soul) and the superego (or government). It is behaviourism if the ego chooses the superego—and it is existentialism if the ego chooses the id. The superego is an object of power and the id is a subject of power. Behaviourism is the model currently used in Western society and only asks that we behave ourselves. It refutes the possibility that any human reality exists outside material appearances.

KIERKEGAARD

Søren Kierkegaard (1813–1855) was a Danish religious philosopher concerned with individual existence and subjective choice who profoundly influenced theology and existential philosophy. He wrote critical works on Christianity, morality, psychology, and religious philosophy. Kierkegaard used metaphors, ironies, and parables. Much of his philosophy deals with how individuals are to live. He focused on actual human reality rather than abstract ideas, emphasizing the significance of personal choice and commitment to one's beliefs. His *Fear and Trembling* book stresses that one must work out one's salvation with "fear and trembling"—i.e., feel the fear and do it anyway. Kierkegaard sought to understand the anxiety that was present with Abraham in the Bible when Abraham believed he was ordered by God to take his own son's life. Kierkegaard also identified the religious sphere as something guided by a devotion to the divine. In his book *Either/Or*, Kierkegaard describes the other two spheres of existence as the aesthetic and the ethical. The aesthetic sphere is a refined form of hedonism that searches for pleasure and the enhancement of mood. The aesthetic individual constantly seeks new experiences in order to stave off boredom and despair; to avoid this, the aesthetic individual must take a leap of faith into the great unknown of an ethical way of life. The ethical sphere involves a passionate embracing of social duties and religious commitments.

NIETZSCHE

Friedrich Nietzsche (1844–1900) was a German philosopher, poet, and philologist. He is perhaps most famous for his claim "God is dead. We have killed Him, you and I." Nietzsche spent much of his career attempting to reaffirm life and counteract nihilism, which called for a radical rethinking of human nature. His book *The Birth of Tragedy* depends on the conflict between the Apollonian and the Dionysian, which are two opposing forces. Apollo is the Greek god of light and reason, and he is characterized by restraint and detachment. Dionysus is the Greek god of wine and dance, and he behaves in a frenzy in which the ego gives way to the self. Both the Apollonian and Dionysian forces are necessary elements for creating value. The first half of the book deals with the nature of Greek tragedy and its relation to Apollonian and Dionysian elements. The second half uses the Greek model to understand modern culture in its decline and its potential rebirth. *Beyond Good and*

Evil is a summary of Nietzsche's mature philosophy. He contrasts other philosophic dogmatisms with his own free spirit. He hoped that future philosophers would be characterized by being willing to follow arguments through to their natural conclusions. Nietzsche also spoke out against the morality of the Everyman, who embodies mediocrity and hates excellence.

DOSTOYEVSKY

Fyodor Dostoyevsky (1821–1881) was a Russian novelist and essay writer, journalist, and philosopher. Dostoyevsky's literary works explore human psychology in the troubled political, social, and spiritual environment of Russia. Many of his works emphasize Christianity and encourage love, forgiveness, and charity as explored by the individual who is being challenged with life's hardships. His book *The Brothers Karamazov* is large in scope and is filled with discussions on faith, doubt, free will, and morality—all topics that inform most of existential philosophy. Broken down into archetypes, Alyosha Karamazov represents the ideal man, Dmitri Karamazov represents the animal in man, and Ivan Karamazov represents the despair of those who rely solely on reason. I would argue that we need both faith and reason to complete the picture; faith is my left hand, and reason is my right hand. Dostoevsky mixes tragedy, philosophy, psychology, drama, and ultimately a hopeful ending into one of the most profound works ever written: *Notes from the Underground*. It tells the story of a former civil servant who embraces a nihilistic view of society. He is sick but refuses medical help, which introduces the notion of perverse freedom. In my own act of perverse freedom, I once sent a letter addressed from "God" to a former employer. When the police arrived on the scene, I tried to convince them they should support the laws of nature as well as the laws of the government. They told me they were not interested in the laws of nature and just wanted to correct my behaviour. The police's behaviour in this instance is an example of behaviourism as the dominant modern paradigm.

KAFKA

Franz Kafka (1883–1924) was an Austrian novel and short story writer. His disturbing fiction anticipated the oppression and despair of the late twentieth century up until today. The term "Kafkaesque" has come to refer to the type of anxious and grotesque social situations that characterize Kafka's work. It emphasizes the loneliness, frustration, and guilt of individuals threatened by nameless forces beyond their control and comprehension. His book *The Trial* is the story of a man occupying the position of chief financial officer of a bank. The man is unpredictably arrested by two agents from an unspecified government agency for an unnamed crime. The nature of his crime is never revealed to him or the reader. His true crime is that he shifts from seeing himself through his own eyes to the eyes of the government. Because of this, he willingly accepts a knife to his heart. *The Metamorphosis* emphasizes a style that blends reality with fantasy and irony. Kafka presents a nightmarish scene in this novel; the protagonist is a hardworking insurance agent who awakens to find he is turning into a huge insect. He remembers nothing of his former self and adapts to new circumstances as they present themselves. He is abandoned by his family and left to die alone.

CAMUS

Albert Camus (1913–1960) was a French-Algerian novelist, essayist, journalist, and playwright. He was awarded the Nobel Prize in literature. Camus addressed the concepts of absurdity and human revolt, and he suggested solutions to the problems of the meaninglessness of modern life. In rebelling against his former friend Sartre, Camus claimed not to be an existentialist. Despite this claim, his *The Myth of Sisyphus* is a profoundly influential work of existential thought. Sisyphus was punished by the gods for deceitfulness and was condemned to spend his life repeatedly pushing a rock up a hill and then watching it roll down. *The Myth of Sisyphus* is a meditation on suicide. Camus answers the question of whether life is worth living in an absurd universe devoid of meaning. Camus concludes by saying that Sisyphus is happy and can live with dignity and authenticity. Camus describes his *The Fall* as mordant, brilliant, and elegantly styled:

"It is a novel of the consciousness of modern man in the face of evil. In a seedy Amsterdam bar named Mexico City, an expatriate Frenchman indulges in a calculated confession. He recalls his past life as a respected Parisian lawyer, a champion of noble causes and, privately, a libertine immune to judgment. As his narrative unfolds, ambiguities amass—every triumph reveals a failure, every motive a hidden treachery. The irony of his recital anticipates his downfall—and implicates us all."

SARTRE

Jean-Paul Sartre (1905–1980) was a French philosopher, novelist, and political journalist. Sartre's philosophic works attempt to combine subjective choice, phenomenology, metaphysics, and the socialism of Marx into a singular view of existentialism. His main conviction is that we are condemned to be free; we are free even if we do not want to be free and tend to flee freedom in bad faith. Sartre was an independent socialist critical of both the Soviet Union and the United States during the Cold War. He declined the offer of the Nobel Prize in literature on principle. In his *Being and Nothingness*, Sartre conceives humans as beings who create the world by rebelling against authority and accepting responsibility for their actions. His book asserts total responsibility for the decisions of individuals. It also made recognition of one's absolute freedom of choice as a necessary condition for human existence. His later book, *Existentialism and*

Human Emotions, is essentially a summary of *Being and Nothingness.* Sartre tells us that we must face the implications of a universe without purpose. Man is responsible for what he is and does. There is no given human nature that he is obliged to fulfill. Man chooses his values and may choose to be an entirely different person at any time.

CONCLUSION

To summarize, existentialism is the philosophy that stresses individual existence, freedom, and choice. It views humans as defining their own meaning in life as beings who try to make rational decisions in an irrational world. Existentialism is all about putting man in touch with himself.

Essay Three:
Existentialism vs.
Behaviourism

This essay argues that a paradigm shift from behaviourism to existentialism is immanent.

Those who hide their complete freedom from themselves out of a spirit of seriousness or by means of deterministic excuses, I shall call cowards.

—Jean-Paul Sartre

O N AUGUST 30TH, 2003, I lost my house and checked into the hospital. Dr. David (his first name) did my intake assessment. The following is an exchange of assessments between Dr. David and myself.

> Patient: Christopher Bek, Physician: Dr. David. August 30th, 2003. Psychotic— paranoid identification. Believes government took his house as not listening to his theories. Diminished ability to care for self. No insight into illness. Flight risk. Becomes agitated when his beliefs are challenged.

> Patient: Dr. David, Physician: Dr. Bek. September 14th, 2003. Psychotic as a result of being out of touch with innate reality. Believes government is omnipotent. Hysterically blind to evidence contradicting behaviourism. Paranoia manifests itself as predatory assessments intended to subvert the truth. Becomes aloof when his authority is questioned.

BEHAVIOURISM: WATSON AND SKINNER

Behaviourism is the psychological theory based on the works of the psychologists John Watson (1878–1958) and B. F. Skinner (1904–1990). The question that behaviourism asks is whether inner thought processes (i.e., consciousness and self-awareness) exist or not. Self-awareness is consciousness recoiling upon itself. Watson did not deny the existence of these thought processes but insisted that they could not be studied because they are not observable. Skinner in turn took behaviourism to its illogical conclusion by arguing that these thought processes do not exist at all. He made the following *a posteriori* argument in his 1971 book *Beyond Freedom and Dignity*: "Consciousness? Can you see it? Measure it? Pass it around? Then how is it different than something that does not exist at all?" Skinner also wrote, "Many anthropologists, sociologists and psychologists have used their expert knowledge to try and prove that man is free, purposeful and responsible. This escape route is slowly being closed as new evidence of the predictability of human behaviour is discovered. Any personal exemption from complete determinism is being revoked as the scientific analysis of individual behaviour progresses."

BAD BEHAVIOURISM

Behaviourism dominated psychology for the first half of the twentieth century. In failing to recognize existentialism, behaviourism has become the *de facto* cognitive model in our society, and it is still in play today. Behaviourism formulates its own models of behaviour based on laboratory experiments (i.e., *a posteriori* models) instead of by mathematics and ontology (i.e., *a priori* models). According to the *Microsoft Encarta Encyclopedia*, "Behaviourism has led to the formulation of a stimulus-response theory of psychology. It has influenced psychology by replacing the machine-driven notion of stimuli-responses with a functional model that accentuates the meaning of conditions for patients. Behaviourism has introduced a research method for the experimental study of patients. It has currently exchanged the mechanical concept of stimuli-responses with a functional concept emphasizing the meaningfulness of stimulating conditions to patients." According to Donald Palmer, "Behaviourism is the theory that only observable, objective features of human activities need to be studied to provide an adequate scientific accounting of behaviour."

DEFINING EXISTENTIALISM

According to the *Microsoft Encarta Encyclopedia*, "Existentialism is the philosophical movement emphasizing individual existence, freedom and choice that has influenced many diverse writers in the nineteenth and twentieth centuries. Because of the diversity of positions associated with existentialism, the term is believed to be impossible to define precisely. Certain themes common to virtually all existentialist writers can however be identified. The term itself suggests one major theme—the stress on concrete individual existence and consequently on subjectivity, individual freedom and choice." *Webster's Dictionary* defines existentialism as "a nineteenth-and twentieth-century philosophy that is centered on the analysis of existence as not exhaustively describable or understandable in scientific terms. It stresses the freedom and responsibility of the individual, the irreducible uniqueness of an ethical or religious situation. Existentialism emphasizes subjective experiences like anxiety, guilt, dread, and anguish."

EXISTENTIALISM: KIERKEGAARD

Kierkegaard and Sartre effectively bookended existentialism. Kierkegaard built the bridge between Georg Wilhelm Friedrich Hegel and existentialism. Hegel argued that the self only exists by being recognized by another being. This was in direct conflict with Kierkegaard, who claimed that the self only exists by being aware of itself. Ontologically speaking, this is known as self-awareness. Kierkegaard was also influenced by Hegel's brand of metaphysics. Metaphysics involves elements beyond the physical, such as consciousness and self-awareness. Kierkegaard believed that reality was subjective. This was confirmed by relativity theory, quantum theory, and my theory of one. For Kierkegaard and Sartre, philosophy was a passionate way of life. Kierkegaard insisted on the importance of subjective action in responding to arguments. Acting on the principles of the self is crucial for arriving at truthfulness. Comprehending a situation from someone subjectively involved in it is often better than an argument for truth put forth by an objective observer.

EXISTENTIALISM: SARTRE

According to Sartre, existentialism is a philosophy for the Superman, whereby existence precedes essence. Again, consider the example of a pen; first came its essence, and then came its existence—the pen's essence is designed on the drawing board, and then it comes into existence. In organized religion, the Everyman is also described by the "essence precedes existence" scenario. Conversely, the Superman arrives on the scene (i.e., existence) and then creates his essence. The question is, does God define man's essence, or does man define his own essence? The Superman has total freedom and total responsibility, while the Everyman has no freedom and no responsibility, other than to behave normally. Sartre put it this way: "The chief effort of existentialism is to face the implications for personal actions in a universe without purpose. That man is personally responsible for who he is and what he does. There are no values external to man and no given human nature which he is obliged to fulfill. Man chooses his values and makes himself—and therefore may choose to be an entirely different person altogether."

EXISTENTIALISM VS. BAD BEHAVIOURISM

The Freudian cognitive model makes the ego (or consciousness) the decision-maker who must choose between the internal values of the inward id, self, or soul, and the external authority of the superego or the government. As discussed above, behaviourism chooses the superego while existentialism chooses the id. Behaviourism is the psychological theory employed throughout Canada contending that all human activity can be known through visible behaviour and appearance— thereby denying the existence of consciousness and the possibility for self-awareness. Whereas the id exists in the eternal-now, the superego merely exists in the now and persists by mimicking the id, thereby fooling the ego. Behaviourism demands the ego submit to the authority of the superego. Existentialism uses the id as a sounding board to provide a moral basis for decision-making. By not specifically arguing for existentialism, the government effectively makes behaviourism the default cognitive model. A lie of omission is still a lie; this is the liar's loophole that I am closing with this book.

ONTOLOGY AND PSYCHOSIS

Ontology is a branch of metaphysics that serves to identify the fundamental dimensions that constitute reality. Ontologically speaking, and according to E. F. Schumacher (1911–1977), "From a base of matter, man has the power of life like plants, the power of consciousness like animals and self-awareness, which is the power of consciousness recoiling upon itself. This power of self-awareness opens up unlimited possibilities for learning, formulating and accumulating knowledge." Behaviourism only recognizes matter while existentialism sees all four ontological dimensions being—matter, life, consciousness, and self-awareness. Psychosis is the mental disorder characterized by an impaired contact with reality. The very definition of behaviourism denies any reality beyond material appearances, thereby making it a recipe for psychosis.

DR. DAVID AND DR. BEK

The 1980 movie *Brubaker* stars Robert Redford, who goes to a prison. After spending time as an inmate, he exposes his true identity as the warden. I have done the same thing by going into the healthcare system as a patient, only to reveal myself as a doctor, in that I have identified behaviourism as the cancer of modern society. In the opening paragraph of this essay, you will see Dr. David's assessment of me, and my assessment of him. Dr. David did my original intake assessment and was also my psychiatrist for five years later on. I have given him copies of my essays and my letters to the government. I even gave him a copy of one of my favourite books in my library of five hundred books, which is entitled *Irrational Man: A Study in Existential Philosophy* (1958) by William Barrett. I also challenged him to debate behaviourism and existentialism, to which he failed to respond. I would argue that patients should be taught the fundamentals of this book. I would also argue for teaching about God, Christ, consciousness, self-awareness, souls, physics, metaphysics, art, and mathematics. Studying this portfolio of topics here may help one become an existentialist.

CONCLUSION

Thus, behaviourism is generally considered a psychological discipline, and existentialism is generally considered a philosophical discipline. I would argue that each should be viewed as both philosophical and psychological disciplines. We are on the cusp of a monolithic paradigm shift from behaviourism to existentialism. Behaviourism empowers the state, while existentialism empowers the individual.

Essay Four:
Applied Existentialism

This essay presents a method of applying existentialism where the reader starts with primary sources of knowledge. It argues that each of us has total freedom and total responsibility for the entire world.

Existentialism is an attempt to gather all the elements of human reality into a total picture of man.

—William Barrett

DOSTOYEVSKY WAS ARRESTED in 1849 for belonging to a literary group that discussed banned books critical of the government. He spent four years in a Siberian prison camp, followed by six years of enforced military service. He was one of twenty prisoners sentenced to be shot at dawn on December 22, 1849. The prisoners' clothes were removed, and they were forced to stand outside naked for twenty minutes. At the last minute, their death sentences were commuted. Some of the men suffered mental breakdowns, while Dostoyevsky did not even remember feeling the extreme cold of the harsh Russian winter. Dostoyevsky embodied applied existentialism, as he lived an existential life.

I HATE NIETZSCHE

In studying existentialism, I suggest starting with writings about, and not by, the great existential philosophers. The reader could begin with PhilosophyMagazine.com and YouTube. He could then move on to beginners' books by authors like Paul Strathern, Donald Palmer, and William Barrett. If he liked them he could go on to the source and read books written by existential philosophers like Nietzsche. Diving headfirst into writers like Nietzsche can be problematic. I try to be consistent and uncomplicated in my writing, while Nietzsche is bombastic and sometimes contradicts himself. He abuses the reader with the intention of forcing him to think for himself. Reading Nietzsche is the metaphysical equivalent of rock climbing; it might

Christopher Bek

be better to start off walking the foothills. And even if the reader were to read and understand all of Nietzsche's books, he would still only know a slice of existentialism. I recommend building the base with writers that talk about the great existential thinkers.

BEHAVIOURISM AND EXISTENTIALISM

As I've mentioned previously, I contend that we are using the behavioural psychological model in Canada. Behaviourism only asks that we behave normally, and it is the sickness that pervades society. It is the theory that human behaviour can be explained in terms of conditioning while ignoring thoughts and emotions. Behaviourism argues that mental disorders can be treated by altering behaviour. Existentialism cures behaviourism by asking each of us to take total freedom and total responsibility for the world. It is the philosophical theory that emphasizes individuals as free and responsible agents determining their own development through acts of free will. Existentialism gives us purpose.

Doctors, just like physicists, are guilty of the agency problem, which is that they have chosen their own wellbeing over the health of the people. An example of the agency problem is where a manager hires more people than he needs in order to elevate his own status. I would argue that doctors are making people sick with behaviourism and are in turn making a killing off this inflicted illness. Like the physicists, who are in denial

34

of my theory of one, the doctors are also in denial of their painfully obvious mistake, which is that they have effectively chosen behaviourism. Behaviourism is the brainchild of a couple of halfwits named Watson and Skinner (discussed in Essay Three). Existentialism is the product of a long history of great thinkers that goes all the way back to Socrates and includes Shakespeare, Kierkegaard, Nietzsche, Dostoyevsky, Kafka, Camus, and Sartre. They all shared the belief that philosophy begins with the acting, feeling, living human being.

EXISTENCE AND ESSENCE

Sartre tells us that for pens, essence precedes existence. But for man, who arrives on the scene and then creates his essence, existence precedes essence. Christianity tells us that man was created in God's image (or essence). Christian man's essence is predefined, and thus his evolutionary curve is flat. He believes he is only required to behave himself, and then he will be admitted into Heaven when he dies. Obeying the Bible and the Ten Commandments is only a facade of morality. Beneath the surface of bourgeois morality, Christian men are having their way with Mother Nature in a crazed feeding frenzy of non-renewable resources. Scientists tell us we only have fifty years of oil remaining. Nietzsche tells us, "My enemies are those who destroy the world without creating themselves." Existential man creates himself while responsibly using the non-renewable resources. His evolutionary curve goes upward to infinity and beyond. With existentialism, there is no predetermined human nature that man is obligated to fulfill. Existential man is thus free to create himself.

FREE WILL AND DETERMINISM

The question of determinism versus free will has been around since Ancient Greece. According to Wikipedia, "Determinism is the philosophical theory that all events, including moral choices, are completely determined by previously existing causes." It is the worldview that the decision to floss one's teeth tonight was determined at the moment of the Big Bang, while free will is the worldview that rejects the idea that determinism applies to the actions of man. The debate between determinism and free will is important in criminal psychiatry. The crucial question is whether the criminal act is the necessary result of a set of previous causes so that the criminal could not help doing what he did—or is the criminal free to do otherwise, and therefore he is responsible? Determinism arises in a society when the government fails to draw a distinction between it and free will. In that Canadian society is strictly deterministic, it could be argued that criminals are not responsible for their criminal actions. According to Skinner, "Many anthropologists, sociologists and psychologists have used their expert knowledge to prove that man is free, purposeful and responsible. This escape route is slowly being closed as evidence of the predictability of human behaviour is discovered. Any personal exemption from complete determinism is being revoked as scientific analysis progresses." As per Skinner, we should empty the prisons because man's actions are predetermined and he had no choice but to break the laws of the government.

BAD FAITH

With existentialism, individuals are free to make choices and cannot escape this freedom no matter the circumstances. The individual always has freedom of choice, even if he must choose in anguish. Bad faith is a key element of existentialism, and is defined as the flight from freedom and responsibility. One flees freedom and responsibility in bad faith by claiming that it is just the way things are, and that they cannot be changed. The other form of bad faith is when a person sets lofty goals but does not make the effort to achieve them. Authenticity, or good faith, is also a key element of existentialism where one's true nature, spirit, and character exist in reality despite overwhelming social pressure to behave otherwise. Perverse freedom occurs, for example, when a person refuses medical help even though it is generally believed to be in his best interests.

DECISION ANALYSIS

According to Wikipedia, "Decision analysis is the discipline comprising the philosophy, theory, methodology, and professional practice necessary to address important decisions in a formal manner." Decision analysis provides a holistic set of tools with which a decision-maker can formulate models representing decisions. Sartre tells the story of a young Frenchman during World War II who must decide whether to avenge his brother's death and join the war effort, or to stay home and look after his mother. Sartre advises the young man to simply decide. Decision analysis is the missing link in which we may employ a formal methodology of making both large and small decisions in the absence of complete information. Value-focused thinking means we have to understand what we value. In risk management, which is closely linked to decision analysis, we identify the acceptable value-at-risk for a given confidence level. I would argue that decision analysis aligns perfectly with applied existentialism.

APPLIED EXISTENTIALISM

I believe the first step forward in applying existentialism to our lives is to build the base by reading material from elementary sources. Then, by comparing and contrasting behaviourism with existentialism, we can see where we have been and where we are going. This will enable us to understand the monolithic freedom we have in creating ourselves. Understanding the difference between free will and determinism in turn captures the essence of existentialism from thirty thousand feet. While decision analysis is not typically associated with existentialism, it teaches us to make good choices in the presence of uncertainty. We should see our lives like works of art; one cannot say that a brushstroke is correct or not, but only that its value is only subjectively revealed in the coherence of the whole work of art. Just like physicists are ignoring my theory of one because it puts them out of business, doctors are making people sick with behaviourism and are getting money from it. The existential revolution could begin by encouraging grade twelve students to take total freedom and total responsibility for the entire world. Some would take up the challenge, while others would not. Ultimately, I sincerely hope that one day, existentialism will be just another core subject taught in high school, just like English and mathematics.

Conclusion

Camus effectively defined philosophical suicide in *The Myth of Sisyphus* as abandoning our soul in exchange for a comfortable life. He also wrote, "The only true philosophical question is that of suicide." Camus concludes by saying we should choose life over suicide. According to Schumacher, "People ask for bread and are given stones. They beg for advice on how to be saved and are told that salvation is an infantile neurosis. They long for guidance on how to live responsibly and are told they are machines, like computers, without free will and therefore without responsibility." Following Schumacher, while at the same time choosing an existential attitude, decidedly means taking a road less travelled. In keeping with Nietzsche's inflammatory style: I love Nietzsche. That is to say, I have a love–hate relationship with Nietzsche.

Essay Five: World Peace

This essay reviews the theory of one and in particular the argument that reality is an illusion, and then follows the trail that we may achieve both eternal existence and world peace by worshipping our souls and embracing existentialism.

We are approaching the time of a major paradigm shift.

    —Stanislav Grof

I **N THE 1999** movie *Election*, a high school teacher stubbornly preaches to his students about the difference between the terms "morality" and "ethics." He then proceeds to have an affair with one of his students. This existential story elucidates the strictly superficial morality of the bourgeois. Bourgeois morality refers to the social class oriented to materialism and hedonism, and to upholding the political and economic interests of the capitalist ruling class. Bourgeois morality is arrived at through the practice of behaviourism and represents the conventional attitudes of the middle class.

REVIEW OF THE THEORY OF ONE

As mentioned previously, the theory of one unites relativity theory with quantum theory by recognizing that light speed and Planck's constant are the same boundary of the universe. Metaphorically speaking, there is no difference between looking through a telescope (relativity theory) and looking through a microscope (quantum theory). It proves the universe is bounded, there is only one photon (that photon is God), and that reality is an illusion.

THE ILLUSION OF REALITY

According to Einstein's relativity theory as described in Lincoln Barnett's 1948 book *The Universe and Dr. Einstein*, "If a stick should attain the velocity of light, it would shrink to nothing at all." Relativity theory is an application of the Pythagorean Form and tells us that as we accelerate towards the speed of light, we begin to shrink in the direction of motion. This means if we reach light speed, we literally exit spacetime. The theory of one then recognizes the velocity of light as a boundary of the spacetime continuum. It is not bounded at some distant star, but the boundary exists right in front of our eyes. We then perceive reality on a four-dimensional screen that surrounds us, where our perception is not only visual but includes all of the senses, including experiencing gravity. It then follows that reality is an illusion, meaning that what we perceive as physical reality is actually an organically generated computer simulation. As Bishop George Berkeley (1685–1753) said, "All the choir of heaven and furniture of earth—in a word all those bodies which compose the mighty frame of the world—have not any substance without the mind. So long as they are not perceived by me, or do not exist in my mind or in the mind of any spirit, they have no existence whatsoever."

PERCEPTION IS REALITY

Physicists believe there are a trillion, billion stars in the universe. The conservation of energy law states that energy can neither be created nor destroyed, and we know from Einstein's $E=mc2$ equation that matter is just a different form of energy. So where did all those stars composed of energy and matter come from?

Saint Augustine (354–430) said, "Miracles happen, not in opposition to nature, but in opposition to what we know of nature." When we turn to look at the moon, the computer in our head accesses the moon's parameters from the hard disk (innate reality) and then calculates and projects the perception of the moon onto a four-dimensional screen (perceived reality) that is the boundary that separates spacetime and nothingness. This screen is also the medium that supports both light and matter waves. Thus, the stars and all of reality are only illusions, and no miracle has actually taken place. Many religions have been saying for centuries that reality is a mirage. The theory of one provides a scientific basis for this belief that reality only exists when a conscious being perceives it. Perception is reality.

SOURCE OF ENERGY

The answer to the question of where energy comes from is that every living being, every blade of grass in the universe is its own energy source. For example, consciousness is a swirling vortex of energy that produces more energy like the interest earned on a mutual fund. To review, the four ontological types of being in the universe are matter, life, consciousness, and self-awareness. The four types of energy in the universe are gravity, electromagnetism, nuclear-weak, and nuclear-strong. Both Freud and Jung adamantly insisted that the energy that operates our minds is no different than the energy that operates the universe. I would argue that the four types of being line up naturally with the four types of energy; matter aligns with gravity, life aligns with electromagnetism, consciousness aligns with nuclear-weak, and self-awareness aligns with nuclear-strong. If we worship our soul, then our being shifts from consciousness to self-awareness, and the fuel that operates our mind transforms from nuclear-weak energy to nuclear-strong energy.

Ultimate Reality

There is a recent article from *Scientific American Magazine* entitled "Are We Living Inside a Computer?" Many of the physicists mentioned in the article believe the possibility that we are living inside a computer. I am arguing that we are living inside an organic computer that is coincident with God. This question as to the ultimate nature of reality is the most fundamental question we can ask. It is not strictly a question for physicists and philosophers, but for all of us. F. S. C. Northrop said, "If one makes a false or superficial beginning, no matter how rigorous the methods that follow, the initial error will never be corrected." I would argue that we have incorrectly based our society on the superficial belief in objective reality, which is clearly disproved by relativity theory, quantum theory, and my theory of one. Reality is subjective, so things do not exist objectively when no one perceives them. Albert Einstein said, "God is the sum total of the laws of nature." I would argue that there exists a Supreme Being who is going through a lot of trouble to create a simulated reality for us. Consider the 1999 movie *The Matrix* and the *Star Trek* franchise, which both present this idea that we may exist in a simulated reality. My question is, what model of reality does God use? The *Star Trek* model tells us that everything is simulated except for our bodies and minds, while *The Matrix* model tells us that everything is simulated except for our minds.

Worshipping the Soul

In that the soul (or self-awareness, or nuclear-strong energy) exists outside spacetime, we can see that souls only contain eternal verities, which are true for all points inside the universe. For example, if we were to steal something, the energy in our soul would diminish because our actions would not be eternally true. Consider the metaphor of the bank account, with energy instead of funds. If, in our lifetime, we do not reflect on the values of the soul, then our actions are not eternally true and our bank account diminishes. If we do the right thing when possible, then our bank account grows. If, when the music stops, our bank account is empty, then our existence comes to an end. Alternatively, if we lived an exemplary, soul-searching life so that we achieve self-awareness, then we would have the option to reincarnate when the music stops. If we listen to the inner voice of the id (existentialism) over the outer voice of the superego (bourgeois morality or behaviourism), we exist eternally. In other words, if we want to play on

God's team, then we must choose existential morality over bourgeois morality, as God is looking for people who make thoughtful, universal-based decisions, and not for yes-men.

EXISTENTIAL MORALITY

Sheldon Kopp's 1972 book *If You Meet Buddha on the Road, Kill Him* offers a fresh, realistic approach to altering one's destiny and accepting the responsibility that comes with freedom. He says that "no meaning that comes from outside ourselves is real. The Buddhahood in each of us has already been obtained and need only be recognized." We ourselves must decide what values— like world peace, the theory of one, and existentialism— are real for us as individuals. Bourgeois morality only asks that we act normally and is the sickness of our society. Existentialism cures bourgeois morality by asking each of us to take total responsibility for the world. The discipline of existentialism gives us meaning in our lives.

CONCLUSION

One might wonder how we can achieve world peace with philosophy and science. The answer is simple. Shifting from bourgeois morality to existential morality means continually reflecting on the soul in every decision we make, regardless of whether it is large or small. The argument here is that good decisions ultimately lead to world peace. Minds exist within spacetime and are made of nuclear-weak energy, while souls exist eternally and are made of nuclear-strong energy. William James said, "Belief in the thing creates the thing." If we believe in our souls, then they exist. We can survive our physical death if we have a soul. It begins by teaching the kids that they must be tuned in to the laws of nature. Einstein said that "God is the sum total of the laws of nature." By recognizing this, people would no longer commit crimes and act against the laws of nature, as they would know that such acts diminish the soul. We could then realize personal peace, which then flows into the great ocean of world peace.

Essay Six:
Forever Jung

This essay starts with Freud's id, ego, and superego—and adds Jung's structure of the psyche, including consciousness, unconsciousness, complexes, and archetypes (such as the shadow and the self).

Modern man has acquired the willpower to carry out his work proficiently without recourse to chanting, drumming or praying. He is able to translate his ideas into actions without a hitch, while primitive man was hampered by fears and superstitions at each step along the way. Yet in maintaining his creed, modern man pays the price in a remarkable lack of introspection. He is blind to the fact that, with all his rationality and efficiency, he is possessed by powers beyond his control that keep him restlessly on the run.

—Carl Jung

A FEW YEARS AGO, I was walking my dogs Camus and Kafka on our daily trek along the precipice and down the hill to the coffee shops. A few blocks from my house, a neighbour came speeding up in her BMW driving on the wrong side of the road. She was screaming at the top of her lungs, saying that I owed her a small amount of money. I told her to back off, but she did not listen. As far as I was concerned, she was having a psychotic break with reality—acting all wild-eyed and crazy. I was worried that she might try to hit me or my dogs with her car. I took a moment to reflect on the situation and decided it was intolerable. I handed the reigns over to my shadow, and he kicked her car door—crushing it like a beer can. She immediately snapped back into reality. In retrospect, I may have overreacted and made the wrong decision. Yet it is comforting to know I have my shadow to take care of me in times of need.

FREUD AND THE ID, EGO, AND SUPEREGO

Freud was a neurologist and the founder of psychoanalysis. Neurology is a branch of medicine that deals with nervous system disorders. Psychoanalysis is one method of treating mental illness through dialogue between patient and psychoanalyst. The bridge between the neurology of human emotions and psychoanalysis is found in the unconscious mechanisms of the mind and soul. The Freudian cognitive model makes the ego (or consciousness) the decision-maker who must choose between the internal values of the id and the external authority of the superego. Behaviourism chooses the superego while existentialism chooses the id.

JUNG AND ANALYTICAL PSYCHOLOGY

Analytical psychology focuses on individuation (or self-awareness), which is the process of integrating opposites like consciousness and unconsciousness while still maintaining their independence, like the Taoist symbols of yin and yang. He considered becoming self-aware to be the essential process in our development. Jung introduced psychological concepts like the archetype, the collective unconscious, complexes, and extroversion, and introversion. Jung said the realization of the self was his life's work. Existentialism taps into the awesome power of the id and makes people better decision-makers by providing a universal perspective on decisions.

THE PSYCHE

The term "psyche" refers holistically to both the mind (consciousness) and soul (unconsciousness). Jung believed that the psyche is whole at birth and during childhood and often becomes fragmented during adulthood—and it may or may not become whole again later in life. The definition of the "ego" is the same for both Freud and Jung; it is the decision-maker of the psyche that chooses which thoughts, feelings, senses, and intuitions to let into the mind. It is because of the ego that we experience the continuity of the psyche from one moment to the next.

Consciousness

Consciousness is the only component of the psyche that is directly accessible to the individual. In speaking of the importance of consciousness in the structure of the psyche, Jung wrote, "In the final analysis, the decisive factor is always consciousness." Consciousness is broken down into thinking, feeling, sensing, and intuiting. There are also the attitudes of extroversion and introversion. Extroverts tend to the external, objective world, and introverts tend to the inner, subjective world. Self-awareness is the process by which consciousness becomes differentiated from others. The goal of becoming self-aware is to know oneself as thoroughly as possible. A person who does not know himself is not self-aware.

Personal Unconsciousness

Experiences that the ego does not admit to the consciousness go into the personal unconsciousness for storage. It is a receptacle that houses psychic material that the ego considers either unimportant or distressing. Dreams access the personal unconsciousness in order to sort out the psychic material and hopefully make it conscious. It sometimes takes years or even lifetimes for the material in the personal unconsciousness to emerge into consciousness. Psychic energy travels back and forth between the ego and the personal unconscious. Psychic energy is no different than the energy that exists in the universe. The theory of one proves that reality is an illusion, and so it is all happening in our minds. The energy in our minds is coincident with the energy in the universe because our minds are coincident with the universe as per the theory of one.

COLLECTIVE UNCONSCIOUSNESS

While Jung's notion of complexes was of major importance in the discipline of psychology, it was his idea of the collective unconscious that put him on the map. It reveals that individuals are linked to their past, including our evolutionary history. The collective unconscious puts the psyche in context of the evolutionary process. It is a latent reservoir of primordial images and signs that lead all the way back to three-and-a-half billion years ago to when the first two amino acids were getting together to begin the glorious assault on the abyss that is evolution. As we progress through life, the psychic material of the collective unconscious tends to become conscious.

Complexes

Complexes are a related group of psychic ideas that are repressed to some degree and may cause psychic conflict that leads to uncharacteristic mental states or behaviours. They are a central pattern of emotions and memories that exist in the personal unconscious and are organized around a common theme. Jung said, "One does not have a complex, the complex has him." In my youth, I developed a need-to-explain complex. As I became self-aware, the complex moved from unconscious to conscious and in turn allowed me to make better arguments and decisions. I am now focused on making arguments that are simple, beautiful, and reasonable. Archetypes—which I describe below—cross over from the collective unconscious into the personal unconscious and become the seeds that grow into complexes.

Archetypes

Archetypes exist in the collective unconscious and are also known as Platonic forms. Plato believed nonphysical forms represent the most accurate reality. Jung spent much of the last forty years of his life studying archetypes. The more important archetypes include the persona, anima, animus, shadow, and self. The persona archetype is the mask we wear in conforming (or not conforming) in our daily lives. It is necessary to survive. Parents sometime project their persona onto their children in an attempt to validate their own way of being. While the persona is the outward face of the psyche, the anima and the animus are the inward faces. The anima is the female side of males, and the animus is the male side of females. People tend to choose mates that most suitably align with their anima or animus.

THE SHADOW ARCHETYPE

While the anima and animus are projections of the opposite sex, the shadow is the projection of the same sex. In some special people, the shadow walks the razor's edge between genius and madness. When the shadow and the ego work in harmony, a person is often highly functional and more alive. A person who suppresses their shadow may act in a civilized manner, but they may also cut themselves off from wisdom, insight, and creativity. A life without a shadow is shallow and out of touch with the inner, subjective self. A strong shadow may overwhelm the ego once in a while, and a person may appear temporarily unstable. Christian teachings are committed to behaviourism, which in turn subdues the shadow. Christians believe that God created man's essence, and his only responsibility is to behave himself. Existentialists believe that man creates his own essence and therefore can use the shadow to take responsibility for his essence. Rejecting the shadow inhibits the personality. The shadow can be of great assistance in times of crisis, as shown by my car-kicking episode.

THE SELF ARCHETYPE

In his 1973 book *A Primer for Jungian Psychology*, Calvin Hall wrote, "The self is the central archetype in the collective unconscious, much as the Sun is the centre of the solar system." It makes a person whole. The self is the inner guiding light and often does not emerge until later in life. Achieving self-awareness depends largely on the cooperation of the ego. The goal man faces in achieving self-awareness requires extreme discipline, constant effort, and determined wisdom. The self makes conscious that which was previously unconscious. Self-awareness is sometimes achieved through the study of dreams. By realizing the self, man experiences less annoyances and hindrances by recognizing their origin in his unconscious. According to Jung, "My life's goal is the realization of the self." D. H. Lawrence said, "Everything that can possibly be painted has been painted, every brush-stroke that can possibly be laid on canvas has been laid on. Then suddenly, at the age of forty, I began painting myself and am fascinated."

CONCLUSION

Thus, starting with Freud's cognitive model (i.e., id, ego, superego), we can see that Jung's structure of the psyche adds to it and lays out the path to self-awareness. Understanding the psyche, consciousness, unconsciousness, complexes, and archetypes are pieces of the puzzle that lead to inner peace and happiness.

The goal of philosophy and science is to replace ignorance with knowledge. Similarly, both Jung and existentialism aim to take that which is unconscious and make it conscious. From this, we may then recognize the permanence of Jung the existentialist in our development.

Essay Seven:
Redefined Existentialism

This essay re-examines existentialism in context of various other disciplines, and argues that we roll them into the one concept of existentialism as the overruling discipline for the human condition.

I am sure that you are all aware of the extremely grave potential for cultural shock and social disorientation contained in this present situation if the facts were suddenly made public without adequate preparation and conditioning.

—2001: A Space Odyssey (1968)

S ARTRE AND CAMUS first met in 1943 at the opening of Sartre's play, *The Flies*. Camus' novel *The Stranger* had been published a year earlier and was considered to be of literary brilliance. Both were well aware of the other's work, and they became fast friends. They shared common interests, including freedom, responsibility, and the absurd, which formed the basis of the burgeoning philosophical discipline of existentialism. As time went by, Sartre became restless that his version of existentialism had failed to take flight, so he tried to merge it with Marxism. Marxism is scientific communism based on social and economic analysis. It asserts that class relations and societal conflict are a means of attaining social transformation. By the end of his life, Sartre had abandoned Marxism. Meanwhile, Camus stayed with existentialism throughout his career. In 1951, Camus produced his book *The Rebel*. Sartre's publication reviewed the book and totally trashed it. Camus was outraged and ended their friendship. Camus wrote, "I am not interested in being a hero. What interests me is being a man."

PREDEFINING EXISTENTIALISM

The principal values of existentialists are freedom and responsibility in an authentically lived life. The existential attitude is the starting point in an existential life characterized by disorientation, confusion, and dread in a seemingly meaningless and absurd world. Many existentialists regard traditional academic philosophies as too abstract for actual human existence, as most do not address the thinking, acting, feeling, living human being.

PHILOSOPHY AND PSYCHOLOGY

Philosophy literally means "the love of wisdom." Psychology is the science of behaviour and the mind, embracing all aspects of consciousness and unconsciousness. Western philosophy is the philosophical discipline of the Western world dating back to the sixth century BC (Ancient Greece). Thales and Pythagoras both practiced philosophy. Philosophy is the scientific study of essential problems concerning subjects that include existence, essence, knowledge, values, reasoning, and languages. Psychology seeks both conscious and unconscious understanding of the human mind. The history of psychology reveals an academic study of the mind and behaviour that also dates back to Ancient Greece. Psychology was derived from philosophy. Psychology was a branch of philosophy until 1875, when it developed as an independent scientific discipline in Europe and North America. The University of Edinburgh currently offers advanced degrees that combine philosophy and psychology. Philosophy and psychology are just different paths directed towards the same objective, which is to know the human condition.

Humanism

Sartre wrote an essay called "Existentialism is a Humanism" in 1946. Humanism is a philosophical and moral stance that emphasizes human values and the support of human beings both individually and collectively. It refers to any system of thought where human dignity and values are paramount. Humanism affirms humans' abilities to improve their lives through the use of reason and ingenuity, as opposed to thoughtlessly submitting to authority and tradition. It is a progressive philosophy of life that affirms our ability and responsibility to live morally sound lives. Humanism helps us achieve personal fulfillment for the greater good of humanity. In today's environment, humanism represents nontheistic life that is centred on the human being. The discipline looks toward philosophy and science rather than the revelations of supernatural sources in order to understand human reality. Humanism benefits both the individual and their fellow human beings.

Decision Analysis

As a review from "Essay Four: Applied Existentialism," decision analysis provides a holistic set of tools with which a decision-maker can formulate decision models for making decisions in the absence of complete information. Value-focused thinking means we have to understand what we value. In risk management, which is closely linked to decision analysis, we identify the acceptable value at risk for a given confidence level. Decision analysis fits perfectly with existentialism, as we are the sum total of our decisions.

THE CARTESIAN COGITO

Sartre believed the Cartesian *cogito*—"I think, therefore I exist"—proves the existence of the self and is the starting point of existential philosophy. He argued that the *cogito* represents the absolute truth of consciousness becoming aware of itself, and that any theory that takes man away from the *cogito* confounds the truth. Any doctrine of probability which is not bound to a truth dissolves into thin air. We must have a firm hold on the true before we consider the probable. The four moments of a probability distribution are the mean, standard deviation, skewness, and kurtosis. We must first nail down the mean (or true) before we even consider the probability associated with the other three moments. And this truth we can grasp directly by reflecting on the subjectivity of the *cogito*.

EXISTENTIAL PSYCHOLOGY

In 1957, Sartre introduced his brief book *Existentialism and Human Emotions*, in which he wrote, "The principle of existential psychology is that man is a totality and not a collection." Existential psychology is founded on existential philosophy and believes that human existence is best understood through the contextual examination of our own experiences; it helps people reclaim their lives by understanding their unconscious minds. Sartre claimed it is about the original choice, while empirical or Freudian psychology claims it is about the original complex. My original choice is to change the world. My original complex is that I have the need to explain myself. This was difficult while growing up, but now it helps me greatly with my writing. Understanding our original choices and original complexes through psychotherapy brings unconscious thoughts into consciousness so that each of us can better understand ourselves as a totality.

STOICISM

Stoicism is a school of Hellenistic philosophy founded in the third century BC by Zeno. It thrived in both the Roman and Greek worlds and lasted until the third century AD. Stoicism represents the path to happiness found in accepting the life given to us. There is support for the viability of stoicism as a psychological therapy. It argues that virtue is sufficient for realizing happiness. It is essentially a philosophy of personal morality driven by its logic and its natural views of the world. Stoicism helps people accept the truth found in their encountered lives. It encourages individuals to not be seduced by the desire for pleasure and the avoidance of pain. The Serenity Prayer written by the American theologian Reinhold Niebuhr perfectly exemplifies stoicism: "God, grant me the serenity to accept the things I cannot change, the courage to change the things I can, and the wisdom to know the difference."

Consciousness

To review, Schumacher defined the four ontological levels of being as matter, life, consciousness, and self-awareness. According to *Microsoft Encarta Encyclopedia*, "No simple, agreed-upon definition of consciousness exists. Attempts to define consciousness have tended to be merely tautological . . . or merely descriptive, such as awareness, sensations, thoughts, or feelings. In spite of this, the subject of consciousness has had a remarkable history and at one time was the primary subject matter of psychology, although it has since suffered an almost complete and total downfall." I suggest that we revive the study of consciousness so that we are positioned to achieve self-awareness.

Redefining Existentialism

The Cartesian *cogito* proves the existence of the self, and it is a cornerstone of existentialism. Sartre's claim that existence precedes essence means that man is free to create his own essence, and is also a cornerstone. The argument that reality is not deterministic and that each of us is condemned to be free is also a cornerstone. The existential belief that each of us has total responsibility for the whole world is also a cornerstone (in regards to these four cornerstones, I am presenting a smorgasbord of ideas here, so the reader may pick and choose in constructing a brand-new existentialism).

Conclusion

Plato constructed his philosophy by taking the best of what other philosophical disciplines had to offer. I would argue that we should take the best of the philosophical disciplines presented here and create a new, refined existentialism. We could set everything in motion by teaching existentialism to the students and then challenging them to take responsibility. I would ask the reader to take the ball and run with it in redefining existentialism. I am willing to debate any physicist regarding the theory of one, and I am willing to debate any doctor regarding this book, *Existentialism Now.*

Quotations

You never change things by fighting the existing reality. To change something, one must build a new model that makes the existing model obsolete.

—Buckminster Fuller

If you tremble with indignation at every injustice, then you are a comrade of mine.

—Che Guevara

Gradually philosophers and scientists have arrived at the startling conclusion that since every object is simply the sum of its qualities, and since qualities exist only in the mind, the whole objective universe of matter and energy, atoms and stars, does not exist except as a construction of the consciousness, an edifice of conventional symbols shaped by the senses of man.

—Lincoln Barnett

If you want immortality, then go out and make yourself immortal.

—Joaquin Miller

Truth is compared in Scripture to a streaming fountain—if her waters flow not in perpetual progression, then they sicken into a muddy pool of conformity and tradition. A man becomes a heretic in the truth; and if he believes things only because his pastor says so, or the assembly so determines, without knowing other reason, though his belief may be true, the very truth he holds becomes his heresy.

—John Milton

When any creativity becomes useful, it is sucked into the vortex of commercialism, and when a thing becomes commercial, it becomes the enemy of man.

—Arthur Miller

Every opinion tends to become a law.

—Oliver Wendell Holmes

Put me on earth again and I would rather be a serf in the house of some landless man than the king of all these dead men that are done with life.

—*Homer*

We are in danger of developing the cult of the Everyman—meaning a cult of mediocrity.

—*Herbert Clark Hoover*

In 1936, the Nobel Prize-winning physicist Johannes Stark and his followers unleashed a newspaper assault in Germany against "Jewish physics," by which he meant theoretical physics, which he contrasted with German or experimental physics.

—*Richard Brennan*

Concern for man himself and his fate must always be the chief interest of all technical endeavours so that the creations of our mind shall become blessings and not a curse to mankind. Never forget this in the midst of your diagrams and equations.

—*Albert Einstein*

Once in Sunday school, while going over the Greek New Testament, I asked a question regarding the meaning of a parable. The headmaster's answer was so utterly confused and convoluted that I actually experienced my first true moment of consciousness—that is, I suddenly became aware with excruciating clarity that he knew nothing at all. From that moment forward, I began to think for myself—or at least knew that I could. I remember clearly the classroom with its windows so high that we could not see out, the desks, the platform on which the headmaster sat, his thin scholarly face, his nervous habits of twitching his mouth and jerking his hands—and then suddenly this profound inner revelation that neither he nor anyone else knew about anything that mattered. It was this threshold moment that was to be the starting point of my liberation from the external world. I knew then for certain that true knowledge could only be arrived at by authentic inner perception, and that all my loathing of religion, as it was taught to me, was at last vindicated.

—Maurice Nicoll

The fate of specialists in any one area of science is to focus more and more narrowly on their special topic, learning more and more about less and less, until eventually they end up knowing everything about nothing.

—*John Gribbin*

Quantum theory serves well as the basis for learned treatises whose pages overflow with the unfriendly symbols of higher mathematics . . . Here too is a glimpse of the scientific theorist at work, pen and paper his implements, as he experiments with ideas. Not the least of his gifts is a talent for reaching valuable conclusions from what later prove to be faulty premises. For his insight is penetrating. Be it a hint here or a clue there, a crude analogy or a wild guess, he fashions working hypotheses from whatever material is at hand, and, with the divine gift of intuition for guide, courageously follows the faintest will-o'-the-wisp till it show him the way toward truth.

—*Banesh Hoffmann*

According to the Cartesian cogito, the one truth that is safe and secure from any doubt is that of my own existence as a conscious subject, thereby introducing subjectivity into modern philosophy.

—*Thelma Lavine*

On a visit to Leningrad some years ago, I consulted a map to find out where I was, but I could not make it out. From where I stood, I could see several enormous churches, yet there was no trace of them on my map. When finally an interpreter came to help me, he said: "We don't show churches on our maps." Contradicting him, I pointed to one that was very clearly marked. "That is a museum," he said, "and not what we call a 'living church.' It is only 'living churches' we don't show." It then occurred to me that this was not the first time I had been given a map which failed to show many things I could see right in front of my eyes. All through school and university I had been given maps of life and knowledge on which there was hardly a trace of the things that I most cared about and that seemed to me to be of the greatest possible importance to the conduct of my life. I remembered that for many years my perplexity had been complete; and no interpreter had come along to help me. It remained complete until I ceased to suspect the sanity of my perceptions and began, instead, to suspect the soundness of the maps.

—*E. F. Schumacher*

No beauty is comparable to the beauty of truth.

—*René Descartes*

The principal concern expressed by the writers of the Renaissance was the need to restore to man the capacities, strengths, and powers of the individual person for which the Dark Ages (430–1630) had denied.

—Thelma Lavine

The only thing worse than suffering an injustice is committing an injustice.

—Plato

Matter, life, consciousness and self-awareness—these four elements are ontologically—that is, in their fundamental nature— different, incomparable, incommensurable and discontinuous.

—E. F. Schumacher

Society attacks people early when they are most helpless.

—Socrates

No one goes to God who does not go through me.

—Christ

While nineteenth-century psychology was busy at work analyzing the conscious mind, psychoanalysis was engaged in explorations of the unconscious mind. Freud felt that consciousness was only a thin slice of the total mind, that like an iceberg, the larger part of it existed below the surface of awareness. Psychologists answered Freud by saying that the notion of an unconscious mind was a contradiction in terms; the mind, by definition, was conscious. The controversy never reached a final conclusion because both psychology and psychoanalysis changed their objective during the twentieth century. Psychology became the science of behaviour, and psychoanalysis became the science of personality.

—*Calvin Hall*

Sartre rightly identified determinism as the primary enemy.

—*Iris Murdoch*

If this discovery is confirmed, it will surely be one of the most stunning insights into our universe that science has ever uncovered. Its implications are as far-reaching and awe-inspiring as can be imagined. Even as it promises answers to some of our oldest questions, it poses others even more fundamental. We will continue to listen closely to what it has to say as we continue the search for answers and for knowledge that is as old as humanity itself, but essential to our people's future.

—President William Clinton

The final theory of everything will undoubtedly be a mathematical system of uncommon tidiness and rigor that accommodates the physical facts of the universe as we know it. The mathematical neatness will arrive first followed by its explanatory power. Perhaps one day physicists will find a theory of such compelling beauty that its truth cannot be denied—truth will be beauty and beauty will be truth. The theory will be, in precise terms, a myth. A myth is a story that makes sense on its own terms, offers explanations of everything we see before us, but can neither be disproved nor tested. This theory of everything will indeed spell the end of physics. It will be the end not because physics has been able to explain everything, but because physics has at last reached the end of all the things for which it has the power to explain.

—David Lindley

I would rather die than give up philosophy.

—Socrates

The one thing that I have learned in a long life is that all science measured against reality is primitive and childlike— and yet it is the most precious thing we have.

—Albert Einstein

Modern man wants neither God nor Christ— for what he desires is simply the authority of the Church. He wants the physical security of bread, the spiritual security of dogma, and the so-called proof of the existence of miracles. To follow God irrespective of the consequences presents too great a risk. The Church offers up a lighter burden. It serves, selects, and explains the truth, forgives sins and bestows upon man the happiness of children. Yet the price is high. Man must surrender his freedom of thought and, indeed, he willingly does so. He no longer serves God as God demands of him, but only as the Church tells him so. God's mysteries and miracles are henceforth monopolized and administered by the Church.

—William Hubben

The other gateway to [universal] knowledge may be opened by further development or elaboration of the unified field theory, on which Einstein labored for the last quarter century of his life. Today the outer limits of man's knowledge are defined by relativity, the inner limits by the quantum theory. Relativity has shaped all our concepts of space, time, gravitation and the realities that are too remote and too vast to be perceived. The quantum theory has shaped all our concepts of the atom, the basic units of matter and energy, and the realities that are too elusive and too small to be perceived. Yet these two great scientific systems rest on entirely different and unrelated theoretical foundations . . . The purpose of [Einstein's] unified field theory is to construct a bridge between them.

—Lincoln Barnett

[Relativity] begins to answer questions such as: Is there a beginning and end to time? Where is the farthest point in the universe? What lies beyond the farthest point? What happened at the point of creation? By contrast, [quantum theory asks] precisely the opposite questions: What is the smallest object in the universe? Can matter be divided into smaller and smaller units without limit? . . . In many ways, these two theories appear to be exact opposites.

[Relativity] concerns itself the cosmic motions of galaxies and the universe, while quantum mechanics probes the subatomic world.

—*Michio Kaku*

The story of relativity tells what happened to science when one provisional theory of space and time yields to another. The story of the quantum tells of adventures which recently befell our theories of matter and radiation, and of their unexpected consequences.

—*Banesh Hoffmann*

The speed of light in a vacuum is one of nature's few universal constants. Special relativity theory established that the speed of light is the universal speed limit. No material object can actually reach this speed. Since any object gains apparent mass as it goes faster, gaining an infinite amount at the speed of light, it would take an infinite amount of energy to accelerate to this speed. By the same token, this would become zero if light could slow down.

—*Ian Marshall and Danah Zohar*

Planck's constant is one of the two most important constants in the whole of modern physics, the other being the speed of light. Max Planck was one of the early founding fathers of quantum physics. His main contributions were the theory that electromagnetic radiation happens in discrete quanta, and the discovery that the size of each quanta is associated with a universal constant, a physical ratio or proportion that stays the same in all circumstances and in all frames of reference.

—Ian Marshall and Danah Zohar

The way in which Plato solved the problems of philosophy was to identify what was true in each of the conflicting philosophies and then marshal these truths into a single, unified, original philosophy of his own.

—Thelma Lavine

I want to know God's thoughts. The rest are details.

—Albert Einstein